ONLINE BUSINESS

THE 4 MAJOR METHODS

"HOW TO MAKE $800 A MONTH AND AVOID THE LIES TOLD BY ONLINE GURUS"

Max Musumali

PREFACE

This booklet is short because you deserve the most precious commodity.

Your time.

That and I don't want to waste my time rambling on about things that can be short and precise.

Spread throughout this booklet are actions you can take to get yourself into the right position when starting your online venture. I strongly suggest you complete all the exercises. You'll understand how valuable they are at the end of it all.

Let's get started.

INTRODUCTION

WHY ONLINE BUSINESS?

Why online business?

You likely already know the answer to this question. In our modern society it's the most cost and time effective way to start a business. Full time or as a side hustle. It's also an easy way to expand your current business with little investment.

It's pretty much the safest way to get your feet wet. Taking all this into account, realize that online business is not necessarily superior to its brick and mortar cousin. They are different but not better or worse than each other.

Online business offers you the chance of location independence and the possibility of building semi-passive income.

You may have heard of a "location independent business". This simply refers to a business where you are not forced to stay in one place. To a lot of young people this sounds like a dream come true. It definitely has its advantages.

The passive income craze has been around for a while. Do work once and collect money of it from then on. Sounds near perfect, especially to the lazy among us.

Most income you can make online is not passive though. It's semi-passive at best. You always have to do some maintenance work and stay ahead of the competition.

The reason there is an $800 on the cover is simple. $800 is a nice little sum. It's not a joke amount of money yet it's not so little that it's not worth it. Depending on your total income it also means that you may need to take tax into consideration.

With tax at 30% that means this guide could also be call 'How to make $560 profit every month online'. That's money that can go towards settling your debt and generally enhancing your life. Most importantly it's a start. If you're ambitious there is no reason you can't build a powerful business like this.

MY STORY

Let me give you a quick overview of my history.

I first considered the idea of starting the online gig 7 years ago. Researching as much as I could on the subject I stared consuming everything that would add to my experience.

Somewhere down the line I got paralysis by analysis. I couldn't pull the trigger. Up until now that still gets on my nerves. We regret not the things we have done but the things we didn't do.

About 2 years ago I finally took the plunge and start putting to use all I had read and learned. Some of it worked, some of it didn't. The market changed so rapidly. Adapting to the new systems ended up becoming a major activity.

Most disappointing was the knowledge shared by so called guru's. The majority of it is really just a fat load of bullshit that leads you to buy more of their products time and time again.

One of the projects I worked on was a membership site for my then boss. It took a lot of work and maintenance. If I wasn't tweaking the site I was cold calling potential customers and running around doing offline marketing.

I was doing everything, even meeting and presenting to very high value clients.

I quickly realized that I was making a product that would make someone else tens of thousands of dollars every year.

At the time I was being paid $220 a month. This would have been increased to a whopping $500 once the "site" was more profitable.

Living in a developing country had something to do with the low pay but the fact was that this website had value. Value which I made but would never be truly compensated for.

So I left.

I'd rather starve doing my own thing then be taken advantage of like that.

The experiences I've had thus far may very well shed light on some issues you're interested in.

Why fail time and time again when somebody else can do it for you?

THE MOST IMPORTANT CONCEPTS

HOW DO YOU ACTUALLY MAKE MONEY ONLINE?

SERVICES

You can offer a service online. This could take the form of a digital service or consulting.

A digital service could end up looking like a software. The hosting you pay for a website is a digital service. So is your monthly subscription to Netflix.

Many times services leverage the fact that you are in expert in a field. Expert means that you have enough knowledge and experience to give a layman advice. You don't need to be brilliant, you just need to be better than the person you're giving advice too.

The monetary value of an online service is hard to gauge because the services could be anything. You could sell a software based service for $5 a month. You could also sell it for $5000 a year if it's worth it.

"If it's worth it" being the major point.

The same principle applies to consulting and coaching services.

PRODUCTS

Selling some sort of product online. This could be something physical or digital like a software, ebook or a pair of shoes.

There are endless numbers of products you could sell but arguably only a few that are best suited to you.

You can make "x" amount of dollars with products. I say x because like for services it really depends on what the market is willing to pay.

ADVERTISEMENT

If you're doing business online chances are you own a website. The website that you provide serves as a traffic point. That means people visit your site on a regular basis.

Where there is significant traffic there is the chance for advertisement.

You can have ads on your website to related products, services, events or other website. The most common form of ads are banner ads and text ads like the ones we see from Google.

Normally adverts pay you on a per click basis. That means you get paid every time someone clicks on the link. There's a huge fluctuation in value here. Some ads will pay you $0.05 while others can pay you up to $30.

AFFILIATE COMMISSION

This is similar to advertisement except that you essentially recommend a product or service to your audience. When your visitors buy said product you get a commission for the sale.

You're kind of like an online salesman.

Depending on the product you're vouching for you can make anywhere from $1 to $2,000 per sale. This depends on how valuable the product or service is in other words how luxurious it is. A book gives you a small commission. A car or gives you a large commission.

Makes sense right?

DONATIONS

For whatever platform and information you are providing, you could ask for donations. Many times it's difficult to monetize what you are doing. For some reason we like free stuff on the internet. We end up getting so stuck in this mentality that our awesome websites don't make any money. Donations are an interesting way around this conundrum.

A lot of people who provide something for free do this.

Humbly, ask for donations that go towards the continued existence of your website. You'd be surprised how much people are willing to give to someone who they truly appreciate.

THE VALUE OF INFORMATION

On the internet the vast majority of the time you are selling information, or at least you use information to drive traffic.

People need a reason to come to your site, people need a reason to buy your product.

We use information to reinforce our prospective customers' needs and wants.

It's not necessary to base your business on information but it is the nature of the internet, it couldn't hurt.

To hammer this point home, think of your favorite blogger. She delivers great content that you love to read. This time around she releases an autobiography. You think, "I enjoy everything else she writes I might as well buy her book".

That's how it works.

You were attracted by the free and great information and when she had a product to sell it was a no brainer for you.

HOW VIABLE IS YOUR IDEA?

Whatever your idea is, it needs to be able to turn a profit over and over again.

So the question is how valuable is your idea to the market?

What are people willing to pay for with regards to your topic of expertise?

Is your product innovative enough for you to grab a market share?

If nobody is willing to pay you for what your business is offering then don't bother. To answer these question you need to pay attention. Make as many observations as possible.

Study how the market has evolved and take an educated guess where it might end up. Most importantly ask those people who you think are your target customers if they want what you're selling.

Many experts would say that you first listen to the needs of a market and then build a product or offer a service. Just make sure your idea solves a problem people are willing to pay to have solved.

TRAFFIC AND CONVERSIONS

In the real world one thing you hear marketers repeated consistently is "location, location, location."

Traffic is the online equivalent of location.

This is when people actually see your site, product or service. Therefore we want as much traffic coming our way as possible, but that's not the end of it.

People need to pay you for something. They need to make the conversion from casual browser to paying customer.

If you have 5000 visits to your site with a 1% conversion rate, that means you get 50 sales. If you have 2000 visits to your site at a 5% conversion rate, then you get 100 sales.

Traffic is important but it means little without conversions.

WHY YOU NEED A PRODUCT OR SERVICE

A long long time ago (10 years to be exact) there existed a basic online business model. Start a website on a specific topic, get a ton of traffic and make money through ads and affiliate marketing.

This doesn't work anymore. Well it does, but pretty much every market has gotten saturated to a degree were you can't depend on others for your income.

You need to sell something of your own whether it's a product or a service.

The profit margin is higher and moreover you develop your personal brand this way. This doesn't mean that you can't use affiliate commission and ads as added revenue streams. It does mean that they are inferior to creating and selling your own product.

Don't be afraid to do it. It only takes some hard work, which you're stuck doing anyway in life. You might as well work for more profit.

MARKETING: THE MOST IMPORTANT THING YOU CAN DO

We have already talked about the importance of traffic.

How do you get that traffic? How do you get customers?

The answer is marketing.

What is your marketing strategy?

A strange reality of the business world is that you can have a bad product that sells well. I'm not recommending you build low quality products. It's just that proper marketing is even more important than what it is you're selling.

Think about the iPhone. It's a high-end phone, beautifully designed and very innovative… the first time around.

Other than that the improvements have been minor and incremental. There is nothing innovative about a screen that's 0.5 inches larger

11

than the last one. Nowadays the IPhone is sold through branding not through innovation.

Sooner rather than later your number one job will not be maintaining a website or creating a product, it will be marketing.

RECAP

1. You're either building a platform, selling a good, a service or any combination of these.
2. Information is the most valuable thing there is.
3. Your idea needs to make you money. There needs to be a market.
4. Traffic is important but conversions are superior.
5. Sell a product or a service ASAP.
6. Marketing will be your number 1 job.

METHOD 1: BLOGS

DEFINITION

Nowadays pretty much every site you see is a niche blog to some degree. It addresses some specific aspects of a wider subject. They cover everything from news, social media, education, dieting and so on and so forth. The value of a blog is in the information that's provided.

The concept is the same as it is in a brick and mortar business, become a specialist. Focus on one or a few things you can become very good at and make your money in that niche.

This is pretty much business basics applied to the internet. Most experts and gurus would advise you to become a specialist in your chosen field, market yourself well and leverage your standing to monetize your website. The vast majority of the time this means using ads and affiliate commission to build an income.

REVENUE STREAMS FOR YOUR WEBSITE

A blog can be a very diverse platform. You can make money using all the methods already pointed out:

- Ads

- Affiliate commission

- Selling a Product or Service

- Donations

ADVANTAGES OF A BLOG

Think of a blog as the basic building block for your online business. It is nearly a necessity to guarantee your success on the internet. You don't have to have one but it's advised you do.

DIVERSITY

Being such a malleable opportunity a blog gives you the chance to branch out in as many ways as you see fit or to do the exact opposite.

BUILDING YOUR BRAND

It straight away goes to work building your brand (if you have some traffic) and makes people take you more seriously.

If your online or offline business has a website as some sort of reference, your customers will take it as a sign that you're serious about business.

SUBTLE ENGAGEMENT

A blog helps you engage visitors and customers who otherwise wouldn't bother communicating with you.

For example, "I have a question about ABC but I won't ask it because it seems like too much of a hustle to contact these people."

Most of us are lazy.

Your site gives them a chance to build a relationship with you without putting in too much effort.

DISADVANTAGES OF A BLOG

A blog doesn't really have any disadvantage as it's more of a starting point but the method behind it can cause some problems:

TIME

Blogs generally take time to gain traction. We'll cover this in depth in a bit.

Don't think that you're going to be one of those superheroes that builds a high traffic site in 6 months.

IT DOESN'T REALLY HAVE ANY MONETARY VALUE BY ITSELF

The site itself is a platform.

If it attracts a good amount of traffic that's great but if it hasn't been, or can't be monetized it doesn't have much value.

A blog is not the end but rather a means to an end. It has no monetary value by itself.

I CALL BULL****: WHAT WORKS AND WHAT DOESN'T.

THE NICHE SITE CONCEPT

Even though we've been talking about blogs what you really want to build is an authority site.

The old school idea of quickly building a small and very specific site is out. The market doesn't respond well to that sort of unthoughtful and low quality product.

Today's consumers are savvier and demand more. Your niche site needs to be someone's favorite. It needs to be someone's number 1 or number 2.

You do that by creating awesome and helpful content, the rest will fall into place (not really but you get the point).

This means that your site will be anything but small. Lots of high quality content is the order of the day.

You are going to end up building a giant repertoire of information, turning your blog and you into an authority in your chosen niche.

16

YOU CAN BUILD A SUCCESSFUL BLOG IN LESS THAN 6 MONTHS

Let's start with the assumption that you are not superman. You will also not be handed an Ironman suit out of the blue in the near future.

People have built successful sites in a short space of time but those people aren't you, so don't base your estimation on their luck and/or brilliance.

There is a guy called Brain Dean who is a Search Engine Optimization Specialist. He can make it happen in 4 months. The difference is that's his job. It's how he makes his ends meat.

I recommend what he has to say about building traffic if you want to know how he does it. Visit him at www.backlinko.com.

Success in the online business world means one thing. "How much money are you making", Nothing else.

A good blog can start making you some $250 - $400 a month at the end of the first year. It takes a significant amount of work to get anywhere above $800.

In fact it takes as much work as a brick and mortar business in some ways.

The time frame you should give yourself for your blog to be hit is 2 years, not less.

Within that time you can build the blog while part-timing. That would give you a nice side income of $800 going upwards. This is particularly true if all you do is depend on ad revenue.

If done right you can pretty much get the same pay that is given for an unskilled. It's not a bad trade-off considering the dynamics involved.

I'm not saying that you can't make tens of thousands of dollars, it's just hard and therefore less likely.

A blog is a terrible way to make money.

BRAIN STORMING SESSION

This really is the beginning.

If you haven't figured out what you are going to specialize in get to it.

Brainstorm on what you're good at.

What are you good at?

What things do people ask your advice on?

What are you passionate about?

What could you start a niche blog on?

Build a list of more than 30 possibilities.

RECAP

1. A blog like any business has a specific focus.
2. Most of the time it is the basic building block of an online business.
3. A blog offers you many attack strategies.
4. You don't make money of the blog.
5. Build an authority site.
6. It will take some time.
7. It's pretty much a crappy way to make money.

METHOD 2: MEMBERSHIP SITES

DEFINITION

A membership site is when your customers are paying to have access to a service, product or platform delivered by your website on a regular basis.

This could be a monthly subscription fee to an online magazine.

The yearly fee you pay for hosting your website is also a good example. Whatever hosting service you use is on a subscription basis. You are paying for 'space' on somebodies server.

Certain communities charge for use of their websites. This could be an exclusive social network or a forum for specialists.

The point is you need to be a paying member to use the service or product.

REVENUE STREAMS

Technically speaking you can make money of all the usual ways if you find a way to incorporate them smoothly into your service.

The major revenue source however always be the subscription your customers pay to gain access to what you offer.

Many people drool about the possibilities and rightly so.

The cheekiest real world example of this is a gym. People pay to use the facilities for an extend period of time like 1 year. They stop training after 2 months. This way a small gym can accommodate a number of customers far beyond its actual capacity. For the owners it's raining cash.

THE ADVANTAGES OF MEMBERSHIP SITES

A membership site has one huge advantage that manifests itself in different ways:

THE NATURE OF THE REVENUE

This is a reoccurring income model.

Once somebody opts into your service you have them hooked for a longer time than usual. This is because as long as said persons wants access to what you're offering they will pay you that subscription.

That one customer becomes a return customer instantly.

All of a sudden you're not only looking at what you can sell once to that customer. Now you start thinking of the life time value of that customer. How much you can make of him or her in the long run.

THE POTENTIAL OF THE METHOD

Too put this into context let's take the example of Unity.

Unity is a graphics and game development software that charges a monthly rate for its use.

Currently this is $75 a month which puts it in as a higher end web-based service. Unity is the in-thing for game developers right now and the community is growing at a rapid pace.

If 30,000 people subscribe to their service that means a revenue of $2.25 million in a month.

Now imagine you were to set up a membership site with a customer base of 300 that charges $15 a month. That's a life changing $4,500 in revenue a month. If done right the vast majority of that revenue is actual profit.

A membership site is most definitely a powerful system if you get it right.

THE DISADVANTAGES OF MEMBERSHIP SITE

Most of the cons of a membership site relate to the logistics of running such an operation, this is what I mean:

THE TECHNOLOGY IS MORE ADVANCED

This is quickly being phased out buy the continuous improvements in web business but is still relevant.

It's a lot more of a hassle to set up such a site. If you're outsourcing the construction to a programmer it will also cost you a pretty penny. Luckily there are a bunch of Wordpress plugins that are making it a lot easier.

THE DAY TO DAY RUNNING

This can suck, big time.

If you have something that is based on a community you have to moderate the discussion. You need to be the sheriff keeping the peace.

Customer care becomes a factor with membership sites as people will always have questions. If you don't love what you're doing or at least have some passion for it, this can be rather draining.

KEEPING IT EVERGREEN

Your membership site needs to be kept up to date. This is a definite and not a maybe.

The best would be to design the site in such a way that right from the beginning the content or service will always be relevant. That notion is of course somewhat of a pipe dream these days but working towards it will keep your customers happy.

This is a mindset you should adapt in all your business endeavors.

I CALL BULL****: THAT DOESN'T MAKE SENSE

Many gurus would advise you to build a membership site that sells the website as a platform for a certain interest group to communicate and exchange ideas.

This is also known as a forum.

Now this is a nice idea but it won't work.

Not in the long run and not with the current standards of the internet. If you are going to charge people to have access to a forum you can't let the forum itself be the sales point.

You need to offer them more than that. Sooner rather than later someone is going to come along and create a free website or just a simple Facebook group that will outshine your venture.

There are no barriers to entry as they say in academics. One of your customers is likely to end up a competitor.

There needs to be something else attached to such a membership site like a product, service or major benefits.

Mike from Colorado has a paid member's area. His site is about starting your own plant nursery. He doesn't charge people to just discuss or make connections. He charges his customers for the sales area that they get access to and loads of information.

Members pay to get access to other gardening enthusiasts who they can wholesale their plants too. They all buy from each other and take up different positions in the supply chain.

It's a clever system. Check it out at http://backyardgrowers.com/ultimate-growers-shortcut/ to see exactly what I mean. This isn't an affiliate link, I just like what he does.

Let your work be really beneficial to your customers. Always deliver on quality.

BRAINSTORMING SESSION

We already outlined some ideas for a blog in the previous model.

Now I want you to think of how you can turn each one of those ideas into a membership site.

Don't leave any idea blank saying "this can't work". If all you can think of is a weak and dumb idea then write it down. At the end, it will help your thinking process.

Ask yourself these questions.

What on this site would I pay for on a monthly basis?

Is there something I can add to the site that will make it a viable membership site?

What are the logistics that need to be put in place to make this happen (members' area, hiring a programmer, etc.)?

Remember, there should be at least 30 ideas.

RECAP

1. A membership site offers access to a service, product or platform on a subscription basis.
2. The subscriptions is the major revenue stream.
3. The income is reoccurring and has great potential to scale.
4. The problem is a membership site is significantly harder to set-up and maintain.
5. You need to offer something of real value to your customer not just a forum.

METHOD 3: EBOOKS

DEFINITION

Ebooks are digitized or electronic versions of books. Pretty simple really.

Only thing is that a lot of ebooks don't actually have a physical equivalent. They can be read on any computing device from a laptop to a tablet to an ereader.

The general format that is used, called .epub, offers a no frills text based document. As of 2014 50% of American have a dedicated device (tablet or ereader) and about 28% had read an ebook. This makes the potential of ebooks exciting as more people get familiar with the tech.

The most notable thing is that ebooks make self-publishing easy. You don't have to fight a war with publishing houses to get people to buy your book anymore.

FICTION VS. NON-FICTION

An interesting conundrum that occurs when talking about ebooks as a potential business is what you can write.

Not what niche do you settle in (at first) but do you write fiction or non-fiction.

The world of internet business is very focused on the practical. What works and what doesn't. This approach for some reason doesn't take fantasy and creativity into account. It always seems to be a 'how to guide' or something.

It's easy to forget that the arts are industries by themselves. Pottery, sculpting, painting, poetry and forms of literature are businesses just like everything else.

If you have a practical skill then obviously non-fiction writing will suit you best. Ebooks however offer those with a more 'creative' knack the opportunity to build a side income and business without becoming to left-brained.

As a rule of thumb we say, "Fiction sells more than non-fiction but non-fiction is easier to sell".

There's an exception to this we'll touch on later.

THE BEST MARKET PLACE FOR EBOOKS

You probably already know what I'm going to say. There is a small website called Amazon. If you write an ebook it's going to end up on kindle sooner or later.

Think of Amazon as a search engine like Google that drives traffic to your products. 'Amazon Kindle Direct Publishing' easily gives you access to a ready and willing market.

You don't need to spend so much time worrying about marketing as Amazon supplements it heavily.

There are other platforms you can use to sell your ebook. Beyond Amazon the first you should think of is your own website. I think that makes the dynamics a bit more complicated but it's entirely possible. Other options include:

- Lulu

- Smashwords

- Scribd

I CALL BULL****: $10,000 WITH EBOOKS EASY?

Look around the web and you'll run into a number of gurus who swear by ebooks. 'You can make $10,000 easy'. I'm not too sure what type of person doesn't raise a skeptical eyebrow when reading stuff like that.

I'LL JUST OUTSOURCE EVERYTHING

Ebooks are a volume based business. You need to pump out a lot of them to make good money.

For some reason lots of people have the notion that one can simply hire Ramesh in Bangalore to write an Ebook for $25, sell the book on Amazon and thus build a business that requires little or no work.

Can this work? Yes but having lived in South East Asia let me tell you one thing. If you are reading this your English is way better than someone from Pakistan, India or the Philippines (though the Filipinos try very hard).

Outsourcing is a tricky situation and every single book you commission needs to be rewritten.

Read that again. Every single book. No exceptions.

That's the difference between the language skills. It's still easier than writing the whole thing yourself but don't kid yourself that it's easy money. This is just like any other business it takes commitment and hard work.

Plus quality is never guaranteed when you outsource.

BIG MONEY EASY

You know the easiest way to make money with ebooks?

Write erotica… smut… porn.

Lots of gurus don't mention this but that might be the closest thing to a guaranteed success you could find with ebooks. It's a way to make short term money but the books have little staying power as they have little value.

If you have a portfolio of 30 erotic short stories and upwards you can (most likely will) make a couple of thousand dollars. So long you targeted you audience right.

Why is this relevant? Many gurus that speak of good money within a short period of time show you charts and cheques. From my experience there are only 2 ways to have such success.

One. You already have an audience and a reputation which you leverage to make the ebook a hit. This is less likely.

Two. You create short erotica ebooks that are well targeted to make short and medium term profit. This is more likely.

I did try writing erotica for some time and I found I didn't have the stamina (no pun intended). I published under a pen name and got tired after 2 books. They did however sell with no effort. It just wasn't my thing.

Now maybe you don't want to write smut and prefer making something that contributes to the world, something with real staying power. That takes work.

It is yet again a volume game that requires intelligent marketing and high quality content. Having your own audience before launching helps tremendously as well.

Addressing a certain target market and doing your market research is a necessity. Do not just write about what you want to hear. Make sure the market wants it.

In short your success in ebooks is determined not only by the book but by the systems and platform that surrounds your book.

You can expect to make anywhere from $30 to $300 a month from one ebook if you pick a good niche and do your marketing right. There's definitely a possibility to do better but let's be pessimistic.

BRAINSTORMING SESSION

Go through your blog site ideas and write down at least 2 possible ebooks you could make for that specific niche. As always ask yourself a couple of questions.

What sub-niche can I write an ebook on?

Are there already some successful examples of similar books (it's a good thing if there are, it shows demand exists)?

Can I write 8,000 to 10,000 words on the topic?

You should do this for all 30 blog ideas. That means a minimum of 60 ebook ideas in total.

RECAP

1. An ebook is simply a digital book.
2. You have the options of fiction or non-fiction
3. The number one marketplace is Amazon.
4. Outsourcing the effort is not that easy.
5. Whatever you write, do some market research first.

METHOD 4: ONLINE SHOPPING (E-STORE)

DEFINITION

Online shopping is where it all started. This is the equivalent to taking a brick and mortar retail or service business and putting it online. You can sell your lawnmowers, paintings and clothes through the internet.

It was pretty much a revolution back in the 90s when all of a sudden a 'mom and pop' store had access to a market way beyond its geographical influence.

This was better than mail marketing because it cut a lot of the costs associated with sending out random letter. Plus you didn't have to be a wizard at copywriting. Combined with an effective postal service this changed the game for business in general.

The nice thing with online shopping is that you can pretty much sell anything these days.

This offers not only a realistic chance of building a business but gives a second avenue for income and marketing if you're already established.

A disadvantage (to some people) is that it is the most hands on method of online business. You actually need to touch real stuff and look after your customers.

YOUR OPTIONS

There are two basic options were online shopping is concerned. You can either build your own platform or use one of the many online stores to sell your products.

BUILD YOUR OWN PLATFORM

Create a website were you sell whatever you have directly to the customer.

This is great because at the end of the day you put in all the effort and you get to keep all the profit. On the flip side it takes a lot of work and requires more technical know-how.

This is not a bad option for a business that is already operational, both for marketing and added sales.

USE SOMEBODY ELSE'S PLATFORM

Simply put your stuff on someone's website to sell.

This tends to work as an integrated solution were you can have a product page. They take care of processing the transaction and deal with the money. You have to make sure that you respond to the order by sending the physical item (if applicable).

For their services these platforms charge a percentage fee off whatever you sell. The major advantage with this is not that it's less work but that they drive traffic to your products.

Marketing is king and someone else is taking care of it for you (to an extent). The best examples of these platforms are:

Amazon – the Mack daddy of online retailers. You can sell anything on amazon. It's always a safe bet and has a ridicules focus on user experience. That's for both sellers and buyers.

EBay – used very much as a market place for second hand goods it is still a solid option. Even though people aren't paying it the attention they did in the past it is still a huge online market place you could take advantage of.

Etsy – This one is interesting because it's a younger company. Young as in only 10 years old. This is a market place for vintage and handmade goods. It's the better alternative for your creative endeavors.

Shopify * – this is less of an online market place and more of a web-solution for your business. The brainchild of a snowboard company, the software helps you set up your online store for a monthly fee.

It helps you track everything you need and is intuitive enough for most people to use. Remember that because this is essentially your own store you still need to market yourself and drive traffic to your site.

THE LOGISTICS

As this is a more hands on business you will need to keep track of your supply chain and logistics. Once you get an order it needs to be processed so that the necessary internal paper work has been taken care of.

Before sending you items you need to make sure they are well packaged.

"If it can shake, it can break".

It would help if the packaging was done in an attractive manner. When sending the package you normally have to involve a third party like USPS, DHL or FedEx.

It is also you responsibility to keep track of the package as it is enroot. This can save you some heartache if anything were to go wrong.

In between, you are likely to communicate with your customers and keep them updated where necessary.

Lastly you need to decide whether you want to restock you inventory since it has just been reduced. So that's:

- Process the order.

- Package the item.

- Send the package.

- Track the package's progress.

- Offer customer service.

- Restock your inventory if needed.

DROP SHIPPING

Drop shipping is a nice little development that has been around for a while now. Uncle Wikipedia defines it as:

"A supply chain management technique in which the retailer does not keep goods in stock but instead transfers customer orders and shipment details to either the manufacturer, another retailer, or a wholesaler, who then ships the goods directly to the customer."

Basically you don't keep stock and you're not responsible for packing and sending products. You send all your stuff to a seller like Amazon and they handle the rest. This can make life so much easier.

The most well-known program that lets you do this is 'Fulfilled by Amazon' or FBA for short.

I'm yet to try this but a number of people have built businesses with monthly revenues of tens of thousands of dollars. The down side is that there is a significant start-up cost. You need to pay for the products first.

For more info on drop shipping you can check out Spencer Haws from www.nichepursuits.com. He's been experimenting with FBA and can give you better info than I can.

UNFORTUNATELY I can't call too much bull**** here because I have less experience with this method.

But don't let anyone lie to you. Estores can be ridiculously labor intensive. I've seen the crud people go through to make this sort of business happen. It takes time, patients and a skill for finding good deals for resale.

Don't try to over deliver on what you're selling. Give your customers exactly what you said you would. Don't mess up on the quality but don't go crazy and give them a bunch of free stuff. With ecommerce that sort of behavior disturbs your profit margins a lot more.

Lastly try your best to gain a competitive advantage. There are so many people getting involved with online shopping because of drop shipping. The competition is getting fierce. It has come to the point where you can actually notice who's an online hustler buy looking at peoples shopping carts in Walmart or Target.

When you see someone buying twenty pairs of basketball shoes at once you know something is up.

Find a way to get access to products the competition can't reach as easily. Then you don't need to worry about your neighbor getting a good deal at a hypermarket. You got a great deal somewhere else! A few brave people do this over www.Alibaba.com. They get their stuff straight from the Chinese manufacturers, reducing costs.

BRAINSTORMING SESSION

Now for this brainstorming session I want you to take the ideas you laid out for you blog.

What products or services could you add that may require a store front?

If the niche is handmade metal bracelets for women, it would make an e-store an easy choice. Take your time and play around with the ideas.

If they sound crazy that's ok. Remember nothing is concrete yet so go as crazy as you want.

Don't forget to do this for all of your 30 blog ideas.

RECAP

1. An e-store is simply the web based version of a store.
2. You can build your own website (e.g. by using Shopify or Wordpress)
3. You can use marketplaces like Amazon, Etsy and Ebay.
4. Most of your work will be dealing with the logistics.
5. Drop shipping is an alternative to Estores.

ROUNDING UP
OTHER WAYS TO START AN ONLINE INCOME

The methods previously mentioned can be considered the more traditional way to start a business and make money online.

These are as relevant today as they ever were but there are others methods you could use. Some of them are less competitive but more complicated. Others are easy but have a ceiling on how much you can earn.

See if one of the following methods peaks your interest.

- Flipping websites (e.g. www.flippa.com)

- Creating online courses (e.g. www.udemy.com)

- Peer-to-peer lending (e.g. https://www.prosper.com)

- Drop Shipping (e.g. Fulfilled By Amazon, FBA, www.amazon.com)

- Video marketing (e.g. www.youtube.com)

- Freelancing (e.g. www.freelance.com, www.mechanicalturk.com)

- Apps and software (e.g. www.playstore.com)

- Designing t-shirts (e.g. www.teespring.com)

This booklet is meant to be short and doesn't have the capacity to cover all these methods. It would however be a good idea if you inform yourself to simply keep an opened mind.

REAL TALK: PASSION

Let's keep things on the straight and narrow. As mentioned throughout this book, building a side income or business doesn't happened overnight.

With most hugely successful persons online, there success was 5 years in the making if not longer.

To keep up with the time and the stress involved you need some passion. I know it sounds like generic advice but it's good. Without it you will lose interest in what you're doing soon enough and you won't be actively seeking for opportunities.

To some degree I feel that many of the projects I've worked on where half-assed because I wasn't passionate enough about the subject. I burned myself out quickly since I was doing things I didn't care about.

Your business idea doesn't need to be something you love to the point where you'd end up in a guerrilla war because of it. You do have to have some zeal for it however.

If you work hard enough you will eventually find success. Passion will help you in finding happiness in the endeavor. There is no sense in doing something that doesn't make you happy.

Lots of people start a business because they feel miserable with their current working life. Don't let yourself feel miserable day in day out. Pursue passion, pursue money, and pursue happiness.

REAL TALK: GRIT

Now passion is nice but it's not enough.

Lots of people preach that passion is an end all to motivation. If you are passionate you are motivated and if you are not motivated enough it means you are not passionate.

Bullshit.

If that's the truth then why do business fail all over the place even though most of them are led by passion mad persons? When it gets hard passion and loving what you do will make it easier.

It's like hitting rock bottom with fluffy pillows cushioning the impact.

You see the thing with that analysis is that you are still going to hit rock bottom, it just won't hurt as much.

As the climb up begins you need to learn to toughen it out.

Sometimes it's just about survival, sometimes it's just about getting there, sometimes it's about doing stuff you don't give a damn about.

Being a person of true grit is one of the greatest advantages you can have in this world. Anything big is built one unit at a time. A journey of a thousand miles has many single steps (cliché, I know).

Tell yourself you will stick to your endeavor and that you won't back out for stupid reasons like:

It's too much work. Well what the hell where you thinking? Of course creating value takes work, or at least value people want to pay for. Create systems that work to your advantage and make things easier for yourself. Backing out should be your last option.

It's taking too long. Seriously? How long have you tried? Is that statement reasonable? If it is then you need to do some serious thinking about what you're going to do next.

If it's not (most of the time it's not) you need to be patient. You also need to grow up because greatness takes time. This is something that you know, you just need to accept it for yourself.

Monitor your progress. Give your business enough time to grow and make some money.

REAL TALK: FOCUS

Focus is the number one productivity technique I have ever come across.

That sounds rather silly but here is my point. It's so easy to get distracted today and the world we live in practically forces us to have our eyes on more goals than we can handle.

Our effort is spread among many things and we never feel like we are giving any one thing our all. It's rare that you find someone who can safely say, "I did as much as I could".

Most of the time that's something we tell ourselves to justify shoddy work. We let ourselves be victims of our inconsistent effort. Ironically the first version of this booklet was full of spelling mistakes. Cleaning it up was annoying but I owed it to myself to produce a better product. All the editing may still not have been enough but I know I put real work into it.

Do one thing at a time.

Give it your all, even if your all doesn't seem good enough. Attack your problem until it is solved. Finish to completion. Aim for perfection but know that it will never be perfect.

If you can focus, you have won a battle that most people don't ever dare attempt in their lives.

Focus on your business. Do not spread your efforts. Give it all the attention it needs. Handling one thing at a time will make you more productive and force a higher quality of workmanship at the same time.

WHAT'S YOUR ONE THING?

Coming to the end the question remains, "what is it you want to do?"

What method of making money online best suits you? You can only decide that by yourself but I will make a suggestion.

Don't build individual online pursuits. Build a platform that leverages on many pursuits in one niche.

Look at your business as a system above anything else. A system that has to be as specific and yet as dynamic as possible to flourish. Integrate as much value into your offers as you can and let it be part of your marketing mindset.

Blow your customers mind.

To translate the jibber jabber.

Imagine you want to start an online business whose niche is African women's hair.

If you don't know, the industry that caters to black women's hair around the world is huge. There are so many aspects you could exploit. For starters you can write an ebook regarding the topic. It's not a bad idea because it kind of makes you look like an expert.

At the same time you could set up a site with a blog where you deliver some free content. Like the best way to go about braiding hair and the newest styles this year.

From the traffic you are driving (both from the site itself and the ebook) you could now sell your own merchandise or recommend affiliate goods.

If there is the possibility of offering your vast knowledge on hair as a consulting service, some of your visitors may be interested. You could eventually hold in-person classes teaching them the practical skills you know.

From one niche you build a platform, a system. Even though you are specializing your streams of income are many because of the possibilities your niche offers you. They all feed of each other, driving traffic and making you an authority in what you do.

This is why you where brainstorming!

To see which one of your ideas can give you the most leverage. The best chance of actually making money doing something you want.

Which one you choose is up to you. BUT be warned. We haven't covered validating your online business idea. You need to make sure there is a market and that people are willing to pay for what you are going to offer.

Take a look at the example from earlier, www.backyardgrowers.com which nicely integrates all the various methods.

My final advice is think big. Try to create a system with an integrated approach. Start small and keep on pushing. At the beginning make it as simple as possible and add what you think is needed in stages. Believe in yourself and in your idea.

Remember traffic is great but conversion is king.

CALL TO ACTION

It's up to you to make your idea a reality. Don't be like me and wait another 5 years before you get started. Jump right in and give yourself a chance.

If you enjoyed this book and think it could be helpful to other people, I'd love it if you would leave an honest review on Amazon so the word can spread as much as possible. Good or bad, so long it's honest.

Of course this is good for me but I genuinely don't want people to struggle the way that I did with starting up online and being taken advantage of.

I thank you for your time and wish you only the best in life.

For freedom, for happiness.

With gratitude,

Max

PS: Visit me at www.ingenuitypool.com and subscribe to my mailing list for great content and updates.

RESOURCES YOU MIGHT LIKE

RECOMMENDED BLOGS.

- Real Entrepreneurship – www.ingenuitypool.com (my site!)

- Copy writing and online business – www.bensettle.com

- Online business and some random stuff – www.30daystox.com

RECOMMENDED PODCASTS.

- Nick Loper's 'Side Hustle Nation' podcast.
www.sidehustlenation.com

- Pat Flynn's 'Smart Passive Income' podcast.
www.smartpassiveincome.com

- Chris Ducker's 'New Business' podcast. www.chrisducker.com

- Spencer Haw's 'Niche Pursuits' podcast. www.nichepursuits.com

OTHER BOOKS BY MAX MUSUMALI

- The Passive Income Lie.

http://www.amazon.com/gp/product/B01593T7M4?*Version*=1&*
entries*=0

Printed in Great Britain
by Amazon